The Joy of Nursery Rhymes

Arranged by Cyril Ornadel.

Yorktown Music Press / Music Sales Limited
London / New York / Paris / Sydney / Copenhagen / Madrid

Exclusive Distributors:
Music Sales Limited
Distribution Centre, Newmarket Road, Bury St Edmunds, Suffolk IP33 3YB, UK.
Music Sales Corporation
257 Park Avenue South, New York, NY 10010, USA.
Music Sales Pty Limited
20 Resolution Drive, Caringbah, NSW 2229, Australia.

This book © Copyright 1994 by Yorktown Music Press / Music Sales Limited
Order No. AM91357
ISBN 0-7119-3616-1

Compiled by Peter Evans.
Music edited by Cyril Ornadel.
Music processed by Ternary Graphics.

Baa Baa Black Sheep

Traditional

© Copyright 1994 Dorsey Brothers Music Limited, 8/9 Frith Street, London W1.

Baa   Baa   Black   Sheep   have you a - ny wool?

Yes sir, yes sir, three bags full. One for the mas - ter and

one for my dame, But none for the lit - tle boy that cries down the lane.

Bobby Shaftoe

Traditional

Diddle, Diddle Dumpling, My Son John

Traditional

Ding Dong Bell

Traditional

Eensy Weensy Spider

Traditional

Frère Jacques

Traditional

Georgie Porgie

Traditional

Girls And Boys Come
Out To Play

Traditional

The Grand Old Duke Of York

Traditional

Here We Go Round The Mulberry Bush

Traditional

2.   This is the way we wash our hands…
3.   This is the way we wash our clothes…
4.   This is the way we dry our clothes…
5.   This is the way we iron our clothes…
6.   This is the way we sweep the floor…
7.   This is the way we brush our hair…
8.   This is the way we go to school…
9.   This is the way we come back from school…

Hey Diddle Diddle

Traditional

Hickory Dickory Dock

Traditional

Hick - or - y, dick - or - y dock, the

mouse ___ ran up ___ the clock. The clock struck one, the

mouse ran down, hick - or - y, dick - or - y dock.

Humpty Dumpty

Traditional

Humpty Dumpty sat on a wall,

Humpty Dumpty had a great fall. All the King's horses and

all the King's men Could-n't put Humpty to-geth-er a-gain.

I Had A Little Nut Tree

Traditional

2. I had a little nut tree
   Nothing would it bear
   But a silver nutmeg and a golden pear.
   I skipped over water,
   I danced over sea,
   And all the birds in the air
   Couldn't catch me.

I Saw Three Ships

Traditional

Jack And Jill

Traditional

Jack and Jill went up the hill to fetch a pail of wa - ter.

Jack fell down and broke his crown, and Jill came tumb - ling af - ter.

Ladybird, Ladybird

Traditional

La - dy - bird, la - dy - bird, fly a - way home, your house is on fire and your chil - dren all gone.

Lavender's Blue

Traditional

2.   Call up your men, dilly dilly,
     Set them to work.
     Some to the plough, dilly dilly,
     Some to the cart.

3.   Some to make hay, dilly, dilly,
     Some to cut corn.
     Whilst you and I, dilly, dilly,
     Keep ourselves warm.

4.   Roses are red, dilly, dilly,
     Violets are blue.
     If you love me, dilly, dilly,
     I will love you.

5.   Let the birds sing, dilly, dilly,
     And the lambs play.
     We shall be safe, dilly, dilly,
     Out of harm's way.

Little Bo-Peep

Traditional

2. Little Bo-Peep fell fast asleep
And dreamed she heard them bleating.
But when she awoke, she found it a joke,
For they were still a-fleeting.

3. Then up she took, her little crook,
Determined for to find them.
She found them indeed, but it made her heart bleed,
For they'd left their tails behind them.

Little Boy Blue

Traditional

Little Jack Horner

Traditional

Lit - tle Jack Hor - ner sat in a cor - ner, eat - ing a Christ - mas pie. He put in his thumb and pulled out a plum and said "What a good boy am I!"

Little Miss Muffet

Traditional

London Bridge Is Falling Down

Traditional

2.   Build it up with iron bars…
3.   Iron bars will bend and break…
4.   Build it up with pins and needles…
5.   Pins and needles rust and bend…
6.   Build it up with penny loaves…
7.   Penny loaves will tumble down…
8.   Build it up with gold and silver…
9.   Gold and silver I've not got…
10. Here's a prisoner I have got…
11. What's the prisoner done to you?…
12. Stole my watch and broke my chain…
13. What'll you take to set him free?…
14. One hundred pounds will set him free…
15. One hundred pounds we have not got…
16. Then off to prison he must go…

Mary Had A Little Lamb

Traditional

2. And everywhere that Mary went,
Mary went, Mary went,
Everywhere that Mary went
The lamb was sure to go.

3. It followed her to school one day,
School one day, school one day,
Followed her to school one day,
That was against the rule.

4. It made the children laugh and play,
Laugh and play, laugh and play,
Made the children laugh and play
To see the lamb at school.

Mary, Mary, Quite Contrary

Traditional

Oh, Dear! What Can The Matter Be?

Traditional

Oh Where, Oh Where Has My Little Dog Gone?

Traditional

Old King Cole

Traditional

Old MacDonald

Traditional

* pigs   ** oink-oink
* ducks   ** quack-quack
* cows   ** moo-moo

Oranges And Lemons

Traditional

Old Mother Hubbard

Traditional

Verses

3. She went to the undertaker's
To buy him a coffin:
But when she came back
The poor dog was laughing.

4. She took a clean dish
To get him some tripe:
But when she got back
He was smoking a pipe.

5. She went to the fishmonger's
To buy him some fish:
But when she came back
He was licking the dish.

6. She went to the tavern
For white wine and red:
But when she got back
The dog stood on his head.

7. She went to the fruiterer's
To buy him some fruit:
But when she came back
He was playing the flute.

8. She went to the tailor's
To buy him a coat:
But when she came back
He was riding a goat.

9. She went to the hatter's
To buy him a hat
But when she came back
He was feeding the cat.

10. She went to the barber's
To buy him a wig:
But when she came back
He was dancing a jig.

11. She went to the cobbler's
To buy him some shoes:
But when she came back
He was reading the news.

12. She went to the seamstress
To buy him some linen:
But when she came back
The dog was a-spinning.

13. She went to the hosier's
To buy him some hose:
But when she came back
He was dressed in his clothes.

14. The Dame made a curtsey,
The dog made a bow;
The Dame said, your servant,
The dog said, "Bow-wow".

Pat-A-Cake, Pat-A-Cake, Baker's Man

Traditional

Pease Porridge Hot

Traditional

Pease por-ridge hot, Pease por-ridge cold, Pease por-ridge in the pot nine days old.

Pop Goes The Weasel

Traditional

Half a pound of two-pen-ny rice, Half a pound of

trea - cle, That's the way the mon - ey goes, Pop goes the wea - sel.

Polly Put The Kettle On

Traditional

Pussy Cat, Pussy Cat

Traditional

Pus - sy cat, Pus - sy cat, Where have you been? I've

been to Lon - don to vis - it the Queen. Pus - sy cat, Pus - sy cat,

What did you there? I fright - ened a lit - tle mouse un - der her chair.

Ring-A-Ring O' Roses

Traditional

Rock-A-Bye Baby

Traditional

Row, Row, Row Your Boat

Traditional

Simple Simon

Traditional

Sing A Song Of Sixpence

Traditional

Skip To My Lou

Traditional

Lou, Lou, Skip to my Lou, Lou, Lou, Skip to my Lou,

Lou, Lou, Skip to my Lou, Skip to my Lou, my dar - ling.

1. Lost my part - ner, What - 'll I do? Lost my part - ner, what - 'll I do?

2. I'll find another one, prettier than you…
3. Little red wagon, painted blue…
4. Can't get a red bird, a blue bird'll do…
5. Cows in the meadow, moo, moo, moo…
6. Flies in the meadow, shoo, shoo, shoo…

There's A Hole In My Bucket

Traditional

2. With what shall I fix it?
Dear Liza, dear Liza,
With what shall I fix it?
Dear Liza, with what?

Three Blind Mice

Traditional

The Muffin Man

Traditional

Tom, Tom, The Piper's Son

Traditional

Twinkle, Twinkle, Little Star

Traditional

Wee Willie Winkie

Traditional

Wee Wil - lie Wink - ie, runs through the town,

Up - stairs and down - stairs in his night - gown. Rap - ping at the win - dow,

Cry - ing through the lock, Are the child - ren all in bed, For now it's eight o'clock?

Yankee Doodle

Traditional

© Copyright 1994 Dorsey Brothers Music Limited, 8/9 Frith Street, London W1.

**Printed and bound in Great Britain by
Caligraving Limited Thetford Norfolk**